Abbey's First Day

Written by: Elizabeth Tracy

Illustrated by: Greg Armstrong

Buddy's World AND FRIENDS

www.buddysworldandfriends.com

Educate yourself about Autism by reading

This book is dedicated to all children with Autism who suffer from being bullied everyday because they show signs of being different. Instead of being a bully, educate yourself about autism and become a FRIEND.

Abbey Bee

After weeks of eager anticipation, Abbey's first day of first grade had arrived.

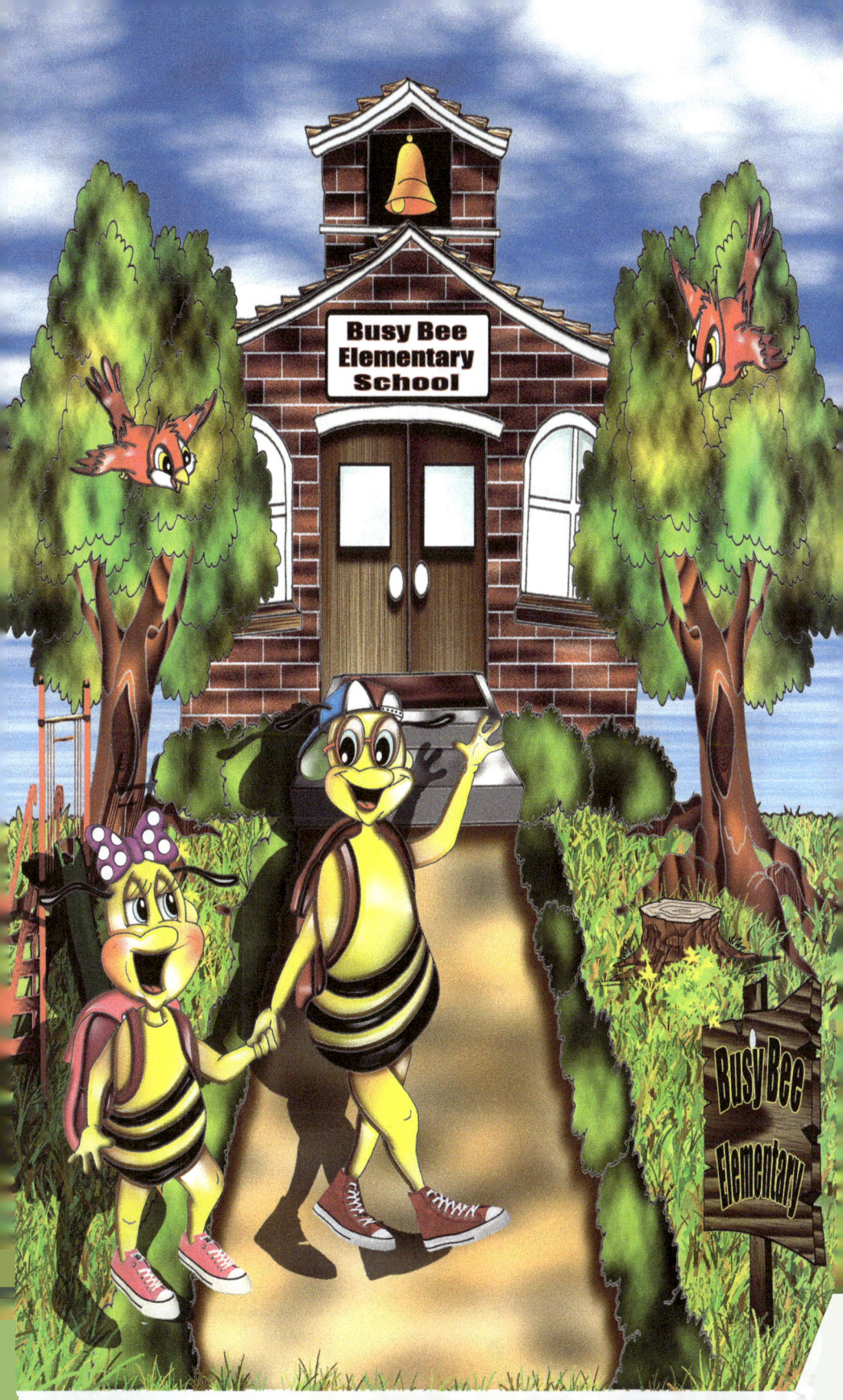

Abbey had flown to the school almost every day to explore the area around it. She was very excited and curious about what she would learn.

Today however Abbey was also a little bit nervous. She had never been away from her parents for an entire day before, so the idea made her anxious.

Abbey's school was beautiful. It was made of red bricks and it had a tall tower containing a large brass bell. A variety of shade trees surrounded the building and behind it was a large playground.

Abbey had played there before she had even learned to fly, swinging on the monkey bars and climbing through the play sets.

Her favorite part, however, was the swing sets. Abbey thought she could swing for hours if she was given the chance. Abbey absolutely loved to swing. It felt like flying, but did not require her to pay close attention to her surroundings.

While swinging Abbey could let her mind wander and stare into space. If she wanted she could stare at the blue sky, fluffy white clouds, and full green trees, but she could also close her eyes, smile and daydream.

The main reason Abbey felt nervous about the start of school was that it would be a major change in her daily routine. Her routine gave her comfort, so the idea of changing it was a bit scary.

Abbey was also nervous because her friend Buddy Bee, whom she had met the previous summer, told her that he sometimes had been bullied when he started school because of his smaller wings. Since having autism made Abbey different as well, she worried that she might be bullied too.

Buddy and Abbey had agreed to meet so they could fly to school together. Abbey was getting nervous because Buddy was running late. When Buddy finally arrived at the agreed upon meeting place, Abbey was pacing back and forth and flapping her hands.

Despite her anxiety, she managed not to show her annoyance with her friend Buddy. Even though she was irritated with him at that moment, she was still glad to see him.

During Abbey's first class her teacher asked which students already knew how to count. Abbey raised her hand first with a huge smile. Miss Bee-a-Teacher called upon Abbey to demonstrate, "Abbey please stand up and count to ten".

Abbey tiptoed to the front of the class with pride. When she turned to face her classmates everyone was staring at her, waiting. Abbey took a deep breath and counted "1,2,3,4,5,6, 7,8,9,10!"

"Wonderful!" exclaimed Miss Bee-a-Teacher. Abbey returned to her seat and listened as every student took a turn practicing just as Abbey had done.

Just as the last bee finished counting a loud bell rang. All of the other bees jumped up from their seats and ran towards the door. "Now,now," Miss Bee-a-Teacher said trying to calm her new students, "It is time for recess. No jumping and stand in a single file line."

The commotion and flood of
excited bees was too much for
Abbey. She buried her head on
desk and covered her head with
a book attempting not to cry.

Once Abbey saw the single file line she was relieved. She liked orderly lines as they reminded her of the time she and Buddy Bee had played in the apple orchad linning up blades of grass from the shortest blade to the longest blade.

Next on the schedule, after recess, was snack time. To help them set good health habits, Miss Bee-a-Teacher first sent the students to the bathroom to wash their hands. They were reminded to wet their hands, apply soap, lather the soap, and rinse.

To dry their hands there were both towels and automatic hand dryers. Most of the students liked how the hand dryers turned on automatically, but Abbey only noticed the noise they made. They were not so loud to others, but there was something about that sound that was almost painful to Abbey's particularly sensitive ears.

Wash your hands
after using bathroom

For a few seconds she waited in line for paper towels, but then she could take it no longer and ran into the hall, almost running into Buddy in the process. "The hand dryers", she replied. " They make the most horrible sound".

Buddy did not know what to do or say. He did not have a problem with the noise, but he understood that Abbey had very sensitive hearing. It made her unique and allowed her to better understand the world around her by hearing things that others could not, but it had it's drawbacks.

Abbey was self-conscious as she returned to the classroom for snack time. She was worried that the students who had seen her act differently around the hair dryer would make fun of her. But as the students filed back into the classroom they all seemed to be talking about recess, and when the teacher brought out the cookies she had made for the class they all focused on snack time.

" See," Buddy said, If any of them noticed what happened by the hair dryer they have already forgotten about it. How about we get some cookies?" That sounds good, Abbey replied.

Abbey's first day was a success despite some challenges. As Buddy and Abbey flew toward their homes Buddy reassured Abbey " Don't worry. Some days you will face challenges at school. Most days will be great!"

About the Author of
Abbey's First Day

Elizabeth M. Tracy is a graduate of The University of Notre Dame class of 2016. _Abbey's First Day_ is Elizabeth's first children's book on Autism Spectrum Disorder. She wrote it as a sequel to her father's book _Buddy Bee's Autism Awareness Adventure_. Elizabeth is "twice-exceptional;" diagnosed with Autism at age three and identified as gifted and talented by 2nd grade. She loves dogs, enjoys cycling and walking and is an accomplished amateur chef.

Life transitions, socialization with peers, and sensory issues have challenged Elizabeth the most. She writes about sensory issues and transition in this book. Elizabeth graduated from high school in Kaukauna, WI as Valedictorian with a perfect 4.0 G.P.A. and scored 34 on the ACT exam. She was involved in many extra-curricular activities from marching and polka band to math club and Rockets for Schools. For two summers Elizabeth attended camp at the U.S. Space and Rocket Center in Huntsville, AL. She earned the prestigious "Right Stuff" Award her first year.

Elizabeth's life changed dramatically upon enrollment at Notre Dame. Her freshman year was respectable. She certainly was not homesick but decided that a major in Engineering did not fit her long-term interests. The coming years brought increased levels of anxiety and indications of agoraphobia. Elizabeth experienced increased sensory overload and often felt overwhelmed by the first quarter of a stimulating Fighting Irish football game. Sleep issues and extreme fatigue ensued. At the beginning of her junior year Elizabeth was diagnosed with a mono-like virus and sat out a semester of college. Once back at Notre Dame Elizabeth continued to struggle for a time with health and academics. At this time Elizabeth enrolled in the University's new Autism Spectrum Disorder Student Success Program. This, in combination with the help of a Life Coach, understanding faculty and staff Elizabeth succeeded and graduated in May 2016. Currently she works on various ASD related projects in her home community and at Notre Dame as a consultant and contributing author to a Peer Mentoring Program Manual.

Author Elizabeth Tracy